George Balanchine: The Life and Legacy of One of the 20th Century's Most Influential Choreographers

By Charles River Editors

About Charles River Editors

Charles River Editors is a boutique digital publishing company, specializing in bringing history back to life with educational and engaging books on a wide range of topics. Keep up to date with our new and free offerings with this 5 second sign up on our weekly mailing list, and visit Our Kindle Author Page to see other recently published Kindle titles.

We make these books for you and always want to know our readers' opinions, so we encourage you to leave reviews and look forward to publishing new and exciting titles each week.

Introduction

"I don't want people who want to dance. I want people who have to dance." - George Balanchine

By the turn of the 20th century, American entertainment was still preoccupied with European-style operetta, as embodied in the works of cellist-composer Victor Herbert. Traditional dance forms moved from European stories to the American prairie in Oklahoma by the late 1940s, and what was once the property of Bavarian princes became the singing standards of cowboys riding through the corn fields in *Oh What a Beautiful Morning and Out of My*

Dreams.

At the time, the availability of classical ballet in America was scant. In contrast to the evolution of an American style in musical theater, Broadway, and film, ballet in the United States was ushered in largely through the efforts of an individual who brought with him a strong traditional sense from Russia and the rest of Europe but was intent on producing a distinctly American style. Other experimentalists appeared, such as Isadora Duncan, but it was George Balanchine who managed to institutionalize and fund both a hybrid traditional as well as experimental form.

Balanchine, although a dancer as well, is today regarded as the "foremost contemporary choreographer in the world of ballet."[1] Despite much work in Russia and other parts of Europe, his eventual relocation to the United States made possible the establishment of an American ballet school and an elite ballet company, the New York City Ballet. In contrast to the fiercely guarded Russian classical style of the Bolshoi Theater, the New York City Ballet featured uniquely choreographed performances to previously unfamiliar musical works. These were approached with a uniquely American style of dance, however steeped in tradition the basic steps may have been.

---

[1] New York City Ballet, George Balanchine – www.nycballet.com/discoveer/our-history/george-balanchine/

George Balanchine: The Life and Legacy of One of the 20th Century's Most Influential Choreographers

Russia

"One is born to be a great dancer." – George Balanchine

George Melitonovich Balanchivadze, widely known today as George Balanchine, was born in St. Petersburg, Russia, on January 22, 1904. The son of a well-known composer and opera singer, Melitone Balanchivadze, his surname was Georgian. His mother was Maria Vasilyeva, a Russian bank employee. Through the years, Balanchine often referred proudly to his non-Slavic ancestry, as the foundations of his art form were distinctly Russian.

Melitone Balanchivadze

Balanchine possessed a gift beyond most of the other famous choreographers from either continent, that of being an advanced musician as well. From 1909, at the age of five, he studied the piano, allowing him to condense thick orchestral scores to fit under the fingers where he could analyze each work privately. This ability was of particular importance in Balanchine's association with the great Russian composer Igor Stravinsky.

Stravinsky

In 1913, at the age of nine, Balanchine enrolled in the Imperial Theater Ballet School in St. Petersburg, joining a group of dancers who spent the subsequent war years in the Imperial School pursuing experimental ballet. He attributed much of his later success to the excellent training he received in Petrograd during those years. At age 11, Balanchine performed on stage for the first time, playing the role of Cupid in Marius Petipa's *The Sleeping Beauty* at the Mariinsky Theater. Petipa went under the moniker of "father of classical ballet."[2] Serving as the favorite work of Balanchine's childhood, he credited that experience with inspiring him toward the pursuit of a ballet career.

Petipa

Petipa, the premiere choreographer in Russia, served as a lifelong inspiration to Balanchine. The Frenchman, who studied in Brussels, introduced a "golden age" of ballet to Russia as the Imperial's *Premier Danseur*. He lived in

Russia for the remainder of his life and became a Russian citizen.

At the age of 16, Balanchine found the opportunity to create his first choreography at the Petrograd Conservatory of Music. Despite his attendance there being devoted to the study of piano and advanced music theory, his studies fit in nicely with his participation in regular recitals in the dance department. While at the conservatory he also studied composition, advanced harmony and counterpoint for the following three years. This advantage allowed him both to remain independent from composers during his study of their works and to speak from the choreographer's and musician's perspective in collaborations with them. As a dancer, Balanchine always took on the character parts rather than a lead role. He increasingly favored choreography in the following years, despite dancing on occasion.

Around the same age, Balanchine mounted his first independent example of choreography entitled *Pas de Deux*, set to the music of Anton Rubinstein entitled *La Nuit* (*The Night*). It was set for two dancers, himself and a female student. Other duets of this period included *Enigma*, to be danced in bare feet, an oddity in the tradition-bound Russian style. In the same year, he created two new ballets for the Mikhailovsky Theater in Petrograd. The 1920 season included his *Le Boeuf sur le*

Toit (The Ox on the Roof), created by Jean Cocteau and composer Darius Milhaud, and a scene from *Caesar and Cleopatra* by George Bernard Shaw.

In the following year after graduating with honors from the Imperial Theater School, he joined the State Theater, formerly known as the Mariinsky Theater, in the corps de ballet. In 1922, Balanchine choreographed performances for the school's graduation, and organized a "small experimental company"[3] called the Young Ballets. In the post-revolutionary period, money was nearly worthless, and Balanchine survived by playing the piano in cabarets in exchange for bread.

Evening classes at the Mariinsky were intended for students not enrolled in the regular daily sessions. Among the students of the evening session was Tamara Gevergeyeva, later known as
Tamara Geva, who went on to become an actress in the United States. Balanchine married her when she had not yet reached the age of 16, although other accounts claim that she was 17. He was 18, and as a lifelong member of the Russian Orthodox Church, two marriage services were held, with the religious service following a civil one. Together, they became part of a nucleus of young dancers that regularly performed his works.

---

[3] The George Balanchine Trust, George Balanchine – www.balanchine.com/george-balanchine/

Geva

Geva became successful as an actress, dancer, and choreographer, with the help of her art patron father, Levko Gevergeyev. She danced in Diaghilev's Ballet Ruses with Balanchine, and in his later American companies. Compiling an impressive filmography, she choreographed several notable Broadway productions. The couple divorced four years later but worked together throughout both of their careers.

In May 1923, Soviet choreographer Fyodor Lopukhov invited Balanchine to work with *Dance Symphony,* a plotless ballet set to the music of Beethoven's Fourth

Symphony, subtitled "Magnificence of the Universe."[4] Lopukhov, despite laboring under the Soviet credo of "social realism,"[5] created "daring choreographic experiments"[6] that proved wildly popular. Participation in this work taught Balanchine a respect for classicism and kindled an interest in experimentation.

Despite Lupokhov's ability to experiment in the face of Soviet oppression, Balanchine found no favor with the state. His non-traditional works were relegated to clubs and a few academic institutions. Of his entire body of work, only *Enigma* remained in the State Ballet's repertory. *Enigma* was set to the music of Anton Arensky. In the 1923 premiere, Balanchine cast himself as the male soloist opposite Lydia Ivanova. Pëtre Gusev recalled that "in this piece for the first time a woman arched into a bridge."[7]

Europe

"God creates, I do not create. I assemble and I steal everywhere to do it - from what I see, from what the dancers can do, from what others do." – George Balanchine

In 1924, Balanchine joined a touring group comprised of

---

[4] Theodore Shabad, Fyodor Lupokhov, Who Guided Russian Ballet's Growth, Dies, N.Y. Times – www.nytimes.com/1973/02.07/archives/fyodor-lupokhov-who-guided-russian-ballets-growth-dies.html

[5] Fodor Lopukhov, Soviet choreographer, Britannica – www.britannica/biography/Frodor-Lopukhov

[6] Fyodor Lopukhov

[7] George Balanchine Foundation, Catalogue, Enigma – www.balanchine.org/balanchine/display-result

principal dancers of the Soviet Ballet. After performances in Germany, the troupe decided not to return home, opting instead to defect. Following an engagement in London, Balanchine traveled to Paris to audition for Serge Diaghilev's Ballet Russes. It was Diaghilev who hired him and changed his name to Balanchine.

Diaghilev

Diaghilev hailed from a wealthy family in Novgorod, and, like Balanchine, he had seriously studied music as a youth, including a regimen of composition study with famed Russian composer Nikolai Rimsky-Korsakov. He also studied painting at the St. Petersburg Academy of the Arts before turning to law. In time, Diaghilev became a special artistic advisor to the Imperial Directorship of Theatres, and to the Mariinsky Theater of St. Petersburg. He was considered "legendary"[8] for linking talented people with wealthy patrons. Balanchine was likely not aware that Diaghilev had his eye on him as a replacement of Bronislava Nijinska as ballet master.

Nijinska was the sister of dancer Nijinsky and a sterling graduate of the Imperial School. Diaghilev suspected she was the best candidate to replace Massinde, who left in 1921. When her brother married and was cast out of Diaghilev's company, she left in solidarity with him, losing her title of "Artist of the Imperial Theaters" and all its associated income.

By this time, Balanchine was suffering a nagging injury to his knee, and his dancing was limited. As the new ballet master of Ballet Russes, he choreographed several productions between 1925 and 1927, and a few for Opera de Monte Carlo. The first was *L'enfant et Sortileges*, the story of a petulant child whose possessions all turn on him. He reworked Léonide Masenes' *Le Chant de Rossignal*, *La Pastorale*, *Jack in the Box*, *The Triumph of*

Neptune and *La Chatte*. As the new choreographer, Balanchine created the first of ten works for Diaghilev, *Barabau*. The ballet was the first to be commissioned from a "witty"[9] original score, but the composer conceived of it before any contact was made with the company. The premiere took place on December 11, 1925, at the Coliseum Theater of London. The score is based on a Tuscan folk melody.

Balanchine's marriage broke apart in 1927. Geva departed to try her hand in American film and Broadway productions, and she was replaced in his affections by Alexandra Danilova. It was no use in attempting a divorce and remarriage, as the amount of paperwork for stateless refugees was an impossible exercise. Still, Balanchine went on to marry four times, each time to a dancer for whom he had created ballets.

---

[9] Reba Adler, Two Versions of Barabau, *Dance Chronicle*, Vol. 4 No. 4 (1981)

Danilova

In the following year, Balanchine choreographed his second ballet to the music of Igor Stravinsky, entitled *Apollon Musagéte*, later renamed *Apollo*. Balanchine regarded *Apollo* as his "artistic coming of age."[10] He claimed that through the creation of this work, he could "dare to use all my ideas, that I too, could eliminate…to the one possibility that is inevitable."[11]

---

[10] The George Balanchine Trust, Apolo

[11] The George Balanchine Trust

A scene from *Apollo*

Stravinsky possessed a strong interest in Greek mythology and composed the score to be danced. At the age of 24, Balanchine received international recognition, and he began a lifetime partnership with the composer.

During the 1928 and 1929 seasons, Balanchine was engaged by the Ballet Russes de Monte Carlo and its founder, René Blum. Blum was a French theatrical impresario who had attained fame as a savior of artwork during World War I. He was the younger brother of the Socialist Prime Minister of France and was later murdered at Auschwitz.

Meanwhile, Balanchine's knee injury became increasingly aggravated, and he toyed with the idea of becoming a pianist, but in the end he opted for choreography instead. He soon immersed himself in the staging of avant-garde theater productions as part of the "artistic ferment swept in by the [Bolshevik] revolution."[12] In 1929, he created a ballet entitled *Le Fils Prodigue (The Prodigal Son)* set to the music of Prokofiev for Diaghilev and the Venice Ballet. Reimagined as a ballet, *Le Fils Prodigue* became a popular early work for Balanchine. It is based on two shocking social phenomena: that a son would ask for his inheritance before his father dies, and the father would forgive his son once the inheritance has been squandered away.

With a choreography "full of bent limbs, fists and acrobatics,"[13] *Prodigal Son* feels jarring even today. Viewers see the son with his drinking buddies, appropriately called "The Goons." The scene is complete with a siren. They all turn on the son in time, holding him upside down and letting the coins fall from his pockets. He ends up at home in his father's arms, assuming the fetal position and enveloped in his cloak. The entire ballet spans 35 minutes and is set to a score by Sergei Prokofiev,

---

[12] Anna Kisselgoff, George Balanchine, 79, Dies in New York, New York Times, May 1, 1983 –
   www.nytimes.com/1983/05/01/obituaries/george-balanchine-79-dies-in-new-york.html

[13] Prodigal Son, George Balanchine Trust – www.balanchine.com/Ballet/Prodigal-Son/

Tamounova

Tamounova was known as "The Black Pearl of the Russian Ballet,"[14] Born on a train as her mother fled Russia, she was raised in refugee camps and lived in Shanghai and Cairo before settling in Paris. Her career lasted an astonishing 40 years, and she eventually found her way to films, including starring with Gregory Peck in *Days of Glory*.

Balanchine eventually left the Ballet Russes, due in large part to the presence of Colonel W. de Basil, who took the

[14] IMDB, Tamara Tamounova (1919-1996) – www.imdb.com/name/nm0869565/

Concurrence, and *Le Bourgeois Gentilhomme. Cotillon* was set to the music of Emmanuel Chabrier, from his *Dix Pièces Pittoresques*. In the story, a cotillion is interrupted by the apparition of a hand gloved in black, the hand of fate. It was performed at the debut program of the company. *La Concurrence* was a single-act piece, also for the opening program, set to the music of George Auric. By the age of 20, Auric had already composed incidental music and orchestrated several ballets. *Le Bourgeois Gentilhomme* was a five-act *comèdie* ballet that poked fun at the pretentious middle class and the aristocracy. A half hour in length, it was set against the music of legendary composer Richard Strauss.

the composer of a famous setting of Romeo and Juliet. However, Diaghilev died that same year, and with that, his company disbanded.

For a few years after, Balanchine undertook various projects around Europe, including engagements with the Royal Danish Ballet. He choreographed one film with former Diaghilev ballerina Lydia Lupkhova, the wife of British economist Maynard Keynes. Trained at the Imperial Ballet School, she toured for some years with the Ballet Russes de Monte Carlo, but an interlude in the United States netted her 18,000 francs per month, 60 times her earnings in Russia. She changed her name to Lopokova and developed a taste for film.

Lopokova

In England, Balanchine created stage extravaganzas for Britain's popular Cochran Musical Theater Revues. Sir Charles Blake Cochran was an English theatrical manager and impresario who produced several of the most popular musical revues, musicals, and theater productions in the 1920s and 1930s. They included productions of Cole Porter and Jerome Kern.

In his work with the Ballet Russes de Monte Carlo, Balanchine discovered a young Tamara Toumanova and created three ballets centered around her talents, *Cotillon*,

Stars and Stripes has been performed on many civic occasions, such as Rockefeller's inauguration as governor of New York and tributes to John F. Kennedy and Lyndon Johnson. The ballet is dedicated to the memory of Fiorella la Guardia, the famous mayor of New York City and founder of the City Center of Music and Drama.

The score is set into five divisions or "campaigns,"[55] with each group of dancers assigned to a "regiment."[56] These were delineated by color of costume, with the American flag in the background. Septime Webre, Director of Washington Ballet and Hong Kong Ballet, suggested that Balanchine "loved America as, I think, only an immigrant can. His ballets are a metaphor for American drive and energy."[57]

Suzanne Farrell, Balanchine's muse and former star member of the company, claimed that "his choreography reflects pure reverence for our country interspersed with light doses of humor, and the pride of belonging and freedom we all share."[58] *Stars and Stripes* was to be used as propaganda by the government, and the State Department set the wheels in motion for the ballet to be toured abroad. Patricia McBride, a dancer who joined the New York City Ballet, cited the book *Balanchine's*

---

[55] The Blog @ The Barre, Stars and Stripes, 7/18/2021 – www.theballetspot.com/the-blog-the-barre/george-balanchine-stars-and-stripes-a-brief-history-of-the-ballet

[56] The Blog @ The Barre

[57] The Blog @ The Barre

[58] The Blog @ The Barre

in a specific order while never repeating. Balanchine recalled that "We constructed every possibility of dividing by twelve."[52] He had reviewed a piece of Arnold Schoenberg at his house the year before, and immediately grasped the dramatic structure. Balanchine wondered why it began and ended with triadic harmony (three-note chord). The two listened again, and out came the inception of Balanchine's ballet *Opus 34*.

By the winter of 1958, President Eisenhower was in the White House and the Korean War was fading from memory. NASA was soon to be founded, and the year's biggest hit was *South Pacific*. On January 17, a new ballet called *Stars and Stripes* was premiered set to the music of John Philip Sousa and Hershy Kaye. The titles of the movements were *Corcoran Cadets*, *Thunder and Gladiator*, *Rifle Regiment Liberty Bell*, *El Capitan*, *The Stars and Stripes Forever*.

The entire production required 41 dancers and was 29 minutes in length, and for all its exuberant patriotic touches, *Stars and Stripes* contains as much "pure dancing"[53] as many full-length classical ballets. Asked why he chose Sousa, Balanchine shrugged and replied, "I like his music."[54]

---

[52] Robert Craft

[53] Stars and Stripes , The George Balanchine Trust – www.balanchine.com/Stars-and-Stripes

[54] Stars and Stripes

10 and 12. He added Arcangelo Corelli's *Saraband* and *Badiniere e Giga,* the second and third movements. The overall work joined the traditions of American folk dance with classical ballets, which Balanchine insisted had "common roots."[48] In the 1957 version, a square dance caller was brought in to call out the steps. Later versions removed the caller and moved the orchestra back into the pit.

Agon was named for the dances of the French court, set to a specifically dance-oriented work of Igor Stravinsky, the composer who helped to fund the production. Stravinsky included specific time directions for the dancers within the score, with a detail of "exact timings"[49] of the basic movements. 12 dancers were clad in simple black and white costumes. At every juncture in their long association, Stravinsky was in an innovate partnership with Balanchine. In a nod to his counterpart's musical background, he openly suggested that "if one wishes to choreograph successfully, then like Balanchine, one must be a musician first.[50]

By the advent of *Agon,* Balanchine was a co-creator with Stravinsky, an "equal partner."[51] A sense of 12-tone music was in the air, in which all 12 tones in the scale are used

[48] Square Dance, The George Balanchine Trust – www.balanchine.com/Ballet/Square-Dance

[49] Agon, The George Balanchine Trust – www.balanchine.com/Ballet/Agon

[50] San Francisco Ballet, Balanchine and Stravinsky: An Innovative Partnership – www.sfballet.org/balanchine-and-stravinsky-an-innovative-partnership/

[51] Robert Craft

and Arnold Schoenberg's *op. 34* in a Stravinsky festival. *Ivesiana* was performed barely four months after the death of the insurance magnate turned modern composer. Complex and atonal, Ives demonstrated considerable skill which Balanchine was able to highlight in an "intense theatricality." The work consists of a string of unrelated orchestral pieces that have been performed only rarely.

Balanchine was fond of saying that his ideas came from the dancers themselves, but he rarely discussed them with the cast. He "invented rapidly and without indulging in fits of temperament."[45] Such a 'cool' approach created a public persona of a "slightly remote and superhuman personality."[46]

Allegro Brillante was staged in 1956 to the music of Tchaikovsky's *Piano Concerto no. 3 in E-flat Major.* It was created for Tallchief and Nicholas Magallanes, but it was later performed exquisitely on film by Suzanne Farrell. It characterized what Tallchief described as "an expansive Russian romanticism."[47]

The following year, Balanchine choreographed *Square Dance*, and *Agon. Square Dance* was set to Antonio Vivaldi's *Concerto Grosso in B minor*, and the first movement of his *Concerto Grosso in E Major, Op. 3*, nos.

---

[45] Katherine Sorley Walker George Balanchine, Russian-American Choreographer, Britannica – www.britannica.com/biography/George-Balanchine

[46] Katherine Sorley Walker

[47] Allegro Brillante, The George Balanchine Trust – www.balanchine.com/Ballet/Allegro-Brillante

choreography and features "brisk footwork and a wistfully romantic pas de deux."[44] The cast included Maria Tallchief, André Eglensky, and Patricia Wilde. The work is 23 minutes in duration and calls for 19 dancers.

Balanchine created his first full-length ballet for the New York City Ballet in 1954 with Tchaikovsky's *Nutcracker*, and it was this production that started the strong winter tradition of Tchaikovsky's *Nutcracker* in America. The source material for the production was taken from Alexandre Dumas' *The Nutcracker and the Mouse King*. Balanchine's enchanting choreography was full of magnificent special effects, including a Christmas tree that grew from 12 feet to 40 feet before the audience's eyes. This evoked audible gasps from viewers at every performance, and the Sugar Plum Fairy was to become one of the most popular mystical figures in all of ballet's history.

On the program as well was the *Western Symphony* of Hershy Kaye, set to traditional American melodies. The physical setting is the rugged West, with cowboys and dancing hall girls, but the production remains classical. Familiar tunes include the *Red River Valley*, *Good Night Ladies*, *Golden Slippers*, and *The Girl I Left Behind Me*.

Balanchine also set *Ivesiana* to the music of Charles Ives

---

[44] Scotch Symphony

for international jokes.

  In 1951, Balanchine choreographed *La Valse* on the music of Maurice Ravel and *Swan Lake* by Tchaikovsky. Ravel's music from *Valses Nobles et Sentimentales* formed the basis for *La Valse*. In his notes on the piece, written during the war years, Ravel wrote, "We are dancing on the edge of a volcano."[40] This is an apt description for Balanchine's choreography that features couples dancing in a "cavernous ballroom."[41] A woman in white is at once horrified and fascinated by the uninvited figure of death, who ultimately claims her life. Diaghilev rejected the work as "un-theatrical"[42] after commissioning it himself, but Balanchine's version effectively rebutted that view.

  The following year was notable for his creation of a ballet called *Scotch Symphony*, set to Felix Mendelssohn's 3rd romantic symphony. Balanchine was "so impressed by the grandeur of the landscape, and the parade of massed Scottish regiments in their stirring "Night Tattoo" that the inspiration was instant. It was his first visit to the Edinburgh Festival, and the splendor was reenacted every night on the castle esplanade. The ballet is considered among the most "charming"[43] examples of modern

[40] La Valse, George Balanchine Trust – www.balanchine.com/Ballet/La-Valse

[41] La Valse

[42] La Valse

[43] Scotch Symphony, NYCB – www.nycballet.com/discover/ballet-repertory/scoth-symphony

Mikhail Baryshnikov.

Balanchine was prone to quote others, possessing a "typically Russian penchant for philosophizing and a verbal wit…that came off as folk wisdom."[33] However, his claim that "Ballet is woman"[34] was pure Balanchine. He added, "The ballet is a purely female thing; it is a woman, a garden of beautiful flowers, and man is the gardener."[35] That sentiment may sound outdated in the present day, but Balanchine insisted that "a woman is inherently worthier than a man"[36] when it comes to ballet. At the same time, he outright rejected any notion that he favored women.

As a professional director, Balanchine fully understood the need for practicality during rehearsal time. He once remarked, "My muse must come on union time."[37] He was also commonly quoted as saying, "There are no mothers-in-law in ballet."[38] His self-observation that "I am not a man, but a cloud in trousers"[39] was particularly effective for attracting the girls. Although he quoted freely from Pushkin, Goethe, Shakespeare, the Bible, the ancient Greeks, Abraham Lincoln, and Paul Valéry, they were rarely original. Throughout it all, he had a particular skill

---

[33] The New Yorker, Balanchine Said – www.newyorker.com/magazine/2009/01/06/balanchine-said
[34] The New Yorker
[35] National Endowment for the Humanities
[36] National Endowment for the Humanities
[37] The New Yorker
[38] The New Yorker
[39] The New Yorker

Balanchine's next major work was *Bourée Fantastique*, set to the music of Emmanuel Chabrier. He had long admired Chabrier's works, discovering them in France after leaving Russia. Balanchine was renowned for his quick wit, "as well as an encyclopedic knowledge of dance forms."[30] In this collection of pieces, he takes aim at many conventions that typify classical dance and offers glimpses of popular dances such as the tango and can-can. *Bourée Fantastique* was large, calling for 42 dancers and performed in four movements. The fourth culminates in a "virtuosic finale,"[31] and it has been described as sharing "a mix of Gallic style, Russian dance vocabulary, and American dynamism."[32] The four movements include the *Marche Joyeuse*, the *Prelude* from the opera *Gwendolyn*, the *Bourée Fantastique*, and the *Fête Polonaise* from the comic opera *La Roi Malgré* (*The Reluctant King*). The cast included two of Balanchine's wives, Tallchief and Le Clercq.

Many have suggested that Balanchine choreographed better for women than he did for male dancers. Even though women enjoy some of the most virtuosic portions of classical ballet, he recruited a wave of great male dancers that served as a rebuttal of that notion, including luminaries like Jacques D'Amboise, Edward Villella, and

---

[30] Bourée Fantastique, NYBC – www.nycballet.co/discover/ballet-repertory/bouree-fantastique

[31] Bourée Fantastique

[32] Bourée Fantastique

proclaimed American dancers as the most beautiful in the world, and he suggested that the best dancers come from the sunnier states of the union. His belief was founded on the American love of sports, most easily enjoyed in the portion of the country with the least rainfall.

On the initial tour, the first performance was postponed due to rain, and the entire tour ended when the manager and exchequer collapsed at virtually the same time. Several versions of the company were created and dissolved, and all efforts ceased during World War II. Kirstein himself served in the Army, while Balanchine went back to Monte Carlo and the Ballet Russe. From Kirstein's and Balanchine's plans for a national ballet company, the only surviving component was the school.

Help came again in the form of Morton Baum. Having witnessed a performance, the enthusiastic Baum transformed the remnants from the war years into the New York City Ballet again. For his act of good faith, Kirstein promised Baum that within three years, he "would give New York City the finest ballet company in America."[29] In 1948, Balanchine added to the company's prestige by inviting Jerome Robbins to join as Associate Artistic Director. Shortly thereafter, Balanchine staged the *Firebird* of Stravinsky, a work to be restaged two decades later by Robbins.

---

[29] NYCB, Our History – www.nycballet.com/discover/our-history/

Following its great success, Morton Baum of the New York City Center of Music and Drama invited Balanchine's troupe to join his organization as a resident ballet company, soon to be renamed the New York City Ballet. Its first performance was held on October 11, 1948.

Once he had assumed the position, Balanchine remained at New York City Ballet for the remainder of his life. It represented a satisfying culmination of his pursuit of professional ballet in America, and he guided it to international prominence.

The idea of what became the New York City Ballet came from Lincoln Kirstein. He knew that Balanchine was the right choice for the directorship, as he was classically trained in the Russian school but was also a bold innovator. Still, the first years of the company were financially stressful. Performances were forced to go as minimalist works, often without any scenery or costumes. From photos, it is evident that a serious ballet troupe would have considerable difficulty emerging in the United States as a display of a "hodge-podge of chubby, self-conscious young women in home one-piece bathing suits."[27] This was soon to be replaced, however, by American dancers with "tall, beautiful long legs."[28] He

---

[27] National Endowment for the Humanities
[28] National Endowment for the Humanities

ask them to do. They have a huge technique."[25] In the first half of the 1940s, Balanchine undertook numerous Broadway shows, including *Rosalina* and *Song of Norway*, which were both operettas. For the Ballet Russe de Monte Carlo, he created several one-act and full-length ballets in the latter years of the decade, including *Danses Concertantes*, *Raymonda*, and *Night Shadow*.

Balanchine took a bit of a hiatus by returning to Europe in 1947. He spent six months as the ballet master of the Paris Opera Ballet. Among his pure dance works were *La Palais de Crital*, which was renamed *Symphony in C* the following year for an American premiere. The work was set to the first symphony of French composer George Bizet, the composer of *Carmen*. It was to be Balanchine's first choreography created for the Paris Opera Ballet. The manuscript had been missing for decades but was discovered in the Conservatory's library. Balanchine choreographed it in a mere two weeks. The *Symphony in C* consisted of four movements, featuring a separate ballerina for each. Following the solo work, the corps of 48 dancers reunite for a "rousing finale."[26]

In the same year, he choreographed *Theme and Variations* for the Ballet Theater, and a version of *Orpheus* written by Stravinsky, a commissioned score.

[25] National Endowment for the Humanities

[26] Symphony in C, The George Balanchine Trust – www.balanchine.com/Ballet/Symphony-in-C

Balanchine in 1942

As a new citizen with such a rate of circulation in high society, Balanchine became an artistic celebrity on par with composer Aron Copland. He believed in Winston Churchill's "special relationship"[24] with the United States and created many examples of patriotic choreography. He countered criticism from overseas ballet institutions with a proud declaration that the Americans don't have a style: "They don't have to do style, they do exactly what you

[24] National Endowment for the Humanities

preoccupied his choice of dance themes, Balanchine increasingly threw himself into historical Americana, including the Western style of dress and increasingly the dance style. Balanchine also enjoyed his new citizenship status, going so far as to say that when he married Maria Tallchief, a Native American, it made him feel as if "he was becoming really American – like John Smith marrying Pocohantas."[21]

By the 1940s, all the ballet institutions that would serve as the predecessors of his future project, The New York City Ballet, were failing. Thus, Balanchine transitioned to the movies, live theater, and operetta to survive. According to a *New York Times* article by Jennifer Dunning, an assistant of Balanchine's named Barbara Hogan held that it was Larry Hart of musical theater fame who really "taught him English."[22] No job was too small in those years. "He did little things, little ballet for big, very wealthy people who had a little ballet in their soiree. He never refused any work that would come."[23]

<hr>

[21] National Endowment for the Humanities, George Balanchine and the United States, Jan./Feb 2016, Vol. 37 No. 1, HUMANITIES

[22] National Endowment for the Humanities

[23] National Endowment for the Humanities

were treated in the coming years to new Balanchine works such as *The Four Temperaments.* That work was set to a score of Paul Hindemith, the company's first commissioned score, and it contained a theme and variations for string orchestra and piano. It was 30 minutes in length, called for 25 dancers, and was based on the medieval belief that all humans are based on the four "temperaments" of earth, air, water, and fire. The movements of the ballet are entitled *Melancholic, Sanguinic, Phlegmatic,* and *Choleric.* Stravinsky's *Rénard* and *Orpheus* shared the program, and the institution went on to become the American Ballet Theater on January 11, 1940.

In 1941, during the work on *Balustrade*, the moment is marked in which the rebirth of Stravinsky's appreciation of the young "Ballet Master" occurred.[20] The change developed during rehearsals for *Orfeo* - before a single note was written, the two had plotted the scenario and the dance numbers. By coincidence, Stravinsky's full realization of Balanchine's musical gifts came about as he watched Balanchine conduct Tchaikovsky for the Ballet Theatre. Clearly, Balanchine could have become a maestro.

Despite the classical and medieval flavors that

---

[20] Robert Craft, Stravinsky and Balanchine, New York Review Oct. 8, 1998 – www.nybooks.com/articles/1998/stravinsky-balanchine/

was called in as artistic director to help revitalize the Ballet Russe de Monte Carlo. In 1941, Balanchine and Kirstein conducted a tour of South America with the American Ballet Caravan that lasted for five months and was bankrolled by Nelson Rockefeller. Unfortunately, the company had no plans for a follow-up slate of performances or more touring, so it disbanded at the end of the journey.

Rockefeller

In 1946, Balanchine and Kirstein, again with the Ballet Society, introduced to New York the concept of subscription-only admission. Audiences who subscribed

with the Metropolitan, which Balanchine described as an "unhappy association."[16] Tight funding for independent dance works only allowed for two completely dance-oriented works, Gluck's *Orfeo and Eurydice* and the all-Stravinsky program. Denouncing the Metropolitan's management for their "conservatism and philistinism,"[17] he took a small group of dancers to the opposite end of the spectrum in Hollywood, choreographing the *Goldwyn Follies*.

In 1938, following his arrival in the United States, Balanchine married Vera Zorina, and following the dissolution of that marriage, he went on to marry Maria Tallchief and Tanquil Le Clercq. With each of his subsequent divorces, he claimed that the women had left him, and each time, he showed an "utter lack of overt emotionalism"[18] that he generally preferred in ballet. When asked, he simply responded by saying, "Some people are hot, and some are cold. Which is better? I prefer cold. I have never cried at a ballet. I never cry anytime."[19]

Balanchine became an American citizen in 1939, during his choreography for the Hollywood film of *On Your Toes*. Between the years of 1940 and 1946, Balanchine

---

[16] Anna Kisselgoff, NY Times

[17] Anna Kisselgoff, NY Times

[18] Anna Kisselgoff, NY Times

[19] Anna Kisselgoff, Ny Times

amount of funding, and in a few months, Balanchine's new project had a brush with financial collapse. Edward M.M. Warburg's support was insufficient to continue, so an invitation to join the Metropolitan Opera as the in-house ballet company was accepted. The first ballet studied and performed at the American school was created by Balanchine and set to the music of Tchaikovsky's *Serenade*. Lacking a traditional ballet venue, it was premiered at Warburg's estate.

As a hybrid experience, The School of American Ballet continued for a time with the Metropolitan Opera, while Balanchine and Kirstein added the first version of an actual ballet company. Balanchine divided his time between this company and his duties as the Met's ballet master. Simultaneously, he began to choreograph for Broadway productions, most prominently the *Ziegfeld Follies: 1936 Edition* and *On Your Toes*. The latter was created for Tamara Geva and Ray Bolger, who played the Scarecrow in *The Wizard of Oz*. *Slaughter on Tenth Avenue* was the most famous portion of that performance, and a few of the dancers also appeared with Ballet Caravan, a small touring company founded by Kirstein in 1936.

In 1937, Balanchine staged the first Igor Stravinsky Festival, to be presented by the American Ballet at the Metropolitan Opera House. At long last, the school split

Balanchine agreed to come to the U.S. almost immediately that year, and he arrived in New York City on October 17, 1933 with the intention of establishing a school to equal or at least rival those of Europe. The result was a national school that trained dancers as young as six and as old as 18. Over 95% of the School of American Ballet's descendant, the New York City Ballet, is manned with graduates. Elsewhere, they commonly appear in the American Ballet Theater, the Boston and San Francisco Ballets, Miami, Pacific Northwest Ballet and the Houston Ballet. This proved the worth of Balanchine's initial insistence that a school come first, to feed the professional companies. Faculty members were comprised of many leading dancers who fled the Russian Revolution. Kirstein openly declared that the school was to provide dancers who were as "well-trained as any other technician, be it surgeon, architect, or musician."[15]

Balanchine's new school first opened its doors on January 2, 1934, at 637 Madison Ave. in New York, with 32 students chosen by audition. A summer program was later established, with a recruiting base of 200 students from across the United States. In recent years, it has provided $2 million in scholarships for these students to train for five weeks in the summer months.

A new ballet school needed a large and consistent

[15] SAB, School of American Ballet – www.sab.org/tyhe-school-and-nycb/

fortune in meeting Edward James, a wealthy dancer from Vienna. Reviews, however, were mixed. Some felt that the company was too youthful, while others considered it too extravagant. Still, Les Ballets underwent several important collaborations, with figures such as Bertold Brecht and Kurt Weill, for whom they choreographed *The Seven Deadly Sins*. Noted composers included Darius Milhaud and Henri Sauget. Artist Paul Tchelitchew was also affiliated. In the end, however, artist tensions pulled the company apart.

America

"Most ballet teachers in the United States are terrible. If they were in medicine, everyone would be poisoned." – George Balanchine

It was around this time that Balanchine met the most important partner of his career, the Boston-born dance connoisseur Lincoln Kirstein. While in London, Kirstein invited him to the United States to establish an American ballet school and company. The two met through the efforts of Romola Nijinsky, the wife of a famous dancer. Kirstein had assisted her in the research for a biography of her husband. A. Everett Austin, Director of the Wadsworth Museum in Hartford, offered institutional sponsorship for a new American school, but both Balanchine and Kirstein declined to work in Hartford.

company away from Blum. Basil, a Soviet director, had served as co-director with Blum, but lost the celebrated dancer Léonid Massine to him as part of a breakaway company working with a U.S. sponsoring agency. He reorganized a company with the remaining dancers called the 'original' Ballet de Russe de Monte Carlo. Balanchine followed this non-Soviet model.

During this period, Balanchine again choreographed for the Royal Danish Ballet, and returned to London to stage dances for another English producer, Oswald Stoll. All in all, he created 107 dances for Stoll, an Australian-born theater manager staging variety shows at the Coliseum, some conducted by his son, Dennis. He also established the annual Royal Variety Performance, a charity presentation to benefit the Artistes' Benevolent Fund. Among Balanchine's most popular contributions was the *Waltz Fantasy in Blue* to the music of Mikhail Glinka, premiered in 1931.

Librettist Boris Kochno and Balanchine founded Les Ballets after both were fired by Colonel Basil. Many new works were produced by the budding choreographer, to music not previously choreographed. The company began in Paris and London, running only four weeks at the Théâtre des Champs-Élysées and at the Savoy Theater. Following the purge by Basil, Toumanova followed Balanchine. The company experienced a burst of good

Ballerinas: Conversations with the Muses, in which Robert Tracy and Sharon De Lano wrote, "Like many emigrés from Soviet Russia, Balanchine was politically conservative and enamored of the American scene."[59]

Farrell

In 1959, Balanchine created *Episodes,* a two-part ballet created that was a collaboration with between Martha Graham and George Balanchine. The music chosen was composed by Anton Webern, his *Symphony op.21, Five Pieces, op. 10, Concerto op. 24*, and the *Ricercata in Six Voices* from *Bach's Musical Offering*, arranged by

---

[59] National Endowment for the Humanities

Webern in homage to Bach. Thirty dancers are employed, and the duration is 27 minutes.

The project grew out of an enthusiasm for Webern's music after it was introduced to Balanchine by Stravinsky. The first time he heard it, he felt as if he were hearing Mozart and Stravinsky together, music that leaves the mind free to "see"[60] the dancing. In Beethoven and Brahms, the music is packed so full of other people's ideas: "How can I …try to squeeze a dancing body into a picture that already exists in someone's mind? It simply won't work. But it will with Webern."[61]

Although the invitation to Martha Graham was to choreograph a joint work, the result was no collaboration. Rather it resulted in a work of two separate sections. The four-part avant-garde work has been performed without Graham's section since. Balanchine's vision varied so greatly from Graham's that "alienation"[62] became a theme – "We…basically cannot tell its head from its feet,"[63] read the New York review.

Tchaikovsky's *Pas de Deux* was created in 1960, along with the *Liebeslieder Waltzes* of Johannes Brahms and *Movements for Piano and Orchestra* of Stravinsky. *The*

[60] Episodes, The George Balanchine Trust – www.balanchine.com/Ballet/Episodes

[61] Episodes

[62] Anna Kisselgoff, New York Times, The Dance: 'Episodes,' June 1, 1986 – www.nytimes.com/1986/06.01/arts/the-dance-episodes.html

[63] Anna Kisselgoff, Episodes

Pas de Deux was originally intended to be part of Act III of *Swan Lake* but was not used. It was composed hurriedly by Tchaikovsky for Bolshoi ballerina Anna Sobeschanskaya who was preparing for a Moscow production in 1877. Rejected in the end from the *Swan Lake* score, it was not published, and disappeared for half a century. The Sobeschanskaya score was rediscovered in the Bolshoi archives in the early 1950s, and Balanchine was granted permission to choreograph it. The 'pas de deux' is a virtuosic tour de force for the dancers, and is "brief, beautiful, and beloved…an adrenaline rush for both the dancers and audiences."[64] The New York City Ballet premiered it on March 29, 1960.

In the same season, the *Liebeslieder Walzer* were created with eight dancers taking on a 49-minute score. Two pianos and a vocal quartet join the dancers on stage. In the first set of 18 waltzes, dancers appear in period ballroom garb. Following a brief lowering of the curtain, the women reappear in ballet dresses with pointe shoes. Throughout the score, romantic associations begin to bloom within the couples.

During this series of triumphs, the School of American Ballet was thriving as well, initiating a series of eight Teachers' Seminars. In these classes, instructors from across the United States came to observe. While a few

[64] New York City Ballet, Tchaikovsky Pas de Deux - www.nycballet.com/discover/ballet-repertory/tschaikovsky-pas-de-deux

took the classes, most sat in a little stand of bleachers. Balanchine personally demonstrated two to four hours per day. Nancy La Salle, patron, trustee, and benefactor asked Balanchine if she could photograph these sessions, and he agreed. A total of 14 photos were released to the public in a book entitled *Balanchine Teaching*. In this book of photographs with accompanying commentary, Balanchine "demonstrated what he thought of as the basics of ballet."[65] Each La Salle photo comes with a brief commentary by Suki Schorer, who danced for Balanchine at the NYCB as the original Butterfly in *The Midsummer Night's Dream*. Schorer later became one of the most honored teachers at the school. She tells us what he is demonstrating, and Balanchine adds a "pleasingly tart teacherly note"[66] at the end of each entry.

As an example, in one photo, Balanchine holds a finger to his nose, sitting in the up and down position and indicating that the body is vertically designed into two halves, left and right. This is to draw a contrast to the Cechetti system, which holds the body should be "divided horizontally, like a stack."[67] This helped Balanchine's dancers appear tall and thin, and he insisted that all dancers do a complete barre every day. "It was like brushing your teeth," he said. "You didn't think about it;

[65] The New Yorker, Balanchine Teaching – www.newyorker.com/culture/culture-desk/balanchine-teaching

[66] The New Yorker

[67] The New Yorker

you just did it."[68] Teaching to Balanchine was, according to him, his main job before choreographing.

In 1962, The New York City Ballet took the enormous step of a tour throughout the Soviet Union. It represented Balanchine's first visit to his native country since he emigrated 38 years earlier, and the production of choice was *A Midsummer Night's Dream*. Shakespeare's legendary play had been used as the source for films and an opera, but it had only been choreographed for dance once, by Frederick Ashton in a one-act entitled *The Dream*. It was to be the first wholly original evening-length ballet Balanchine would choreograph in America.

The work deals with the "transforming power of love."[69] This was accomplished by means of adventures and misadventures, quarreling and reuniting of two pairs of mortals and the King and Queen of the fairies. The music of Felix Mendelssohn on the story was not long enough, and Balanchine studied the composer's other works at length and selected other overtures, a nocturne, an intermezzo, and a portion of the Ninth Symphony to weave together into an entire ballet score.

Before the end of 1962, Balanchine co-created *Noah and the Flood* to the music of Stravinsky with Jacques D'Ambois. It was a ballet expressly intended for

---

[68] The New Yorker

[69] Midsummer Night's Dream, The George Balanchine Trust – www.balanchine.com/Ballet/A-Midsummer-Night's-Dream

television, and involved members of the New York City Ballet, students of the American School of Ballet, and the New York City Opera Chorus. Actor John Houseman served as the narrator. Voice parts were designated for both God and Satan. The original prologue and arietta of Satan was omitted from the score.

Stravinsky's *Movements for Piano and Orchestra* was premiered on April 9, 1963, as a neoclassical ballet. Stravinsky told Balanchine that the music could have easily been titled "Electric Currents." The composer added that experiencing the first performance was like "a tour of a building for which I had drawn the plans but never explored the result."[70] Paired with a newly created *Monumentum pro Gesualdo* for the performance, the company retained the arrangement for future performances. The original cast included Suzanne Farrell and Jacques d'Amboise. *Monumentum pro Gesualdo* is a tribute to the 400th birthday of the 16th century's most chromatic and scandalous composer – a nobleman accused of murder. Stravinsky orchestrated several of Gesualdo's vocal madrigals.

Balanchine created *Bugaku* in the following season as a tribute to the refined elegance of Japanese music and dance. The project originated from two visits to Japan by

---

[70] Movements for Piano and Orchestra, NY City Ballet – www.nycballet.com/discover-ballet-repertory/movements-for-piano-and-orchestra

the NYBC five years earlier, as well as trips to America made by the Gugaku Company of the Imperial Household. Balanchine commissioned a 25-minute score a year before the premiere from Toshero Mayuzumi and set it for a cast of 10 dancers. The music was intended to suggest the Bugaku form but in Western instrumentation. The red, green, and white colors of the setting, "balanced dances"[71] to the left and right, stylized movement, a "ritualistic mood,"[72] respect shown for the dance and the "supreme courtesy"[73] from dancer to dancer are faithful to the Gugaku tradition.

The New York City Ballet moved into its new home, the New York State Theater at Lincoln Center for the Performing Arts in 1964. The new hall was designed by Philip Johnson in consultation with Balanchine and Kirsten. Planning for Lincoln Center had begun in the mid-1950s. Within one decade, six theaters, a library and museum, a fountain, and landscaped parks replete with modern art were completed.

---

[71] Bugaku. The George Balanchine Trust – www.balanchine.com/Ballet/Bugaku
[72] Bugaku
[73] Bugaku

A picture of the New York State Theater

The NYCB's Theater, now renamed the David H. Hoch Theater, is home for the New York City Ballet and serves as a second venue for the American Ballet Theater. It was once home for the New York City Opera, and another defunct tenant was the Music Theater of Lincoln Center with President Richard Rodgers of Rodgers & Hammerstein fame. The theater seats 2,586 and sports four balconies.

A Midsummer Night's Dream opened in America on April 24, 1964 in New York during the company's first repertory season. Fond of the play since a childhood production in which Balanchine played an elf, he could still recite large portions of the play in Russian and had the recent Soviet tour in his immediate memory.

Balanchine's juxtaposition of Mendelssohn's music was recreated with the former additions, beginning with the overture he wrote at the age of 17. An immense cast of 81 were engaged for the broad roster of roles, and the running time for the entire production was 91 minutes.

Despite not dancing for many years, Balanchine undertook the title role of Don Quixote in a 1965 opening. He was 61 years of age. The female lead, Dulcinea, was danced by Suzan Farrell, then 19 years of age, "a dancer with whom he was deeply – madly – in love."[74] The audience included Jerome Robbins, Leonard Bernstein, Leontyne Pryce, and John D. Rockefeller III. Tanaquil Le Clercq, then Balanchine's wife and a former NYCB dancer, was there as well, wheelchair bound after being struck with polio.

[74]Jennifer Homans, Balanchine: Making and Being Don Quixote, The New York Review, June 4, 2015 – www.nybooks.com/articles/2015/06/04/balanchine-making-being-don-quixote

Balanchine and Farrell in *Don Quixote*

Despite his remaining skill and imaginative performance instincts, one critic asked, "What did his theatrical display of feelings for Farrell mean for him? How could he do this to LeClercq who left him for good that night, unable to live with the public humiliation of such a public declaration?"[75]

On the *Don Quixote* program was *Harlequinade*, a new choreography set to the *Pas de Deux* from *Les Millions d'Arlequin* of Riccardo Drigo, a composer from Padua, Italy. Originally danced by Maria Tallchief and André Eglevsky, Balanchine staged the entire work in two acts.

---

[75] Jennifer Homans

On April 12, 1966, Balanchine offered up a romantic work arranged by a modernist composer. The music of the *Brahms-Schoenberg Quartet in G minor* was originally a Piano Quartet by Johannes Brahms. Schoenberg arranged it for chamber orchestra, and explained why in a letter to Dr. Alfred Frankenstein, San Francisco critic. His first justification was that he loved the piece, the second that it is seldom played. The third was that it is always played badly, and one can never hear the strings through the overly loud piano. As Balanchine put it, "I wanted for once to hear everything."[76] It premiered two years after the NYCB moved to Lincoln Center.

Balanchine soon choreographed his first full-length plotless ballet, *Jewels*, to the music of three disparate composers. The first was Gabriel Fauré, a French romantic who was the teacher of Maurice Ravel. The other two were Stravinsky and Tchaikovsky. Balanchine was inspired to create the work by the artistry of jewelry designer Claude Apels. In *Emeralds*, a gem that Balanchine considered "an evocation of France,"[77] the 19th century dances of the French romantics are recalled. *Rubies* has been described as "crisp and witty,"[78] epitomizing the collaboration of Balanchine and Stravinsky. *Diamonds* recalls the "order and grandeur"[79]

[76] Brahms-Schoenberg Quartet – www.balanchine.com/Ballet/Brahms-Schoenberg-Quartet

[77] Jewels, The George Balanchine Trust – www.balanchine.com/Ballet/Jewels

[78] Jewels

[79] Jewels

of Imperial Russia and the Mariinsky Theater, where he was trained.

Final Years

"If you don't feel challenged, it's because you're not doing enough." – George Balanchine

Balanchine created an oddly titled work in 1970 entitled *Who Cares?* Short vocal numbers of George Gershwin arranged by Hershy Kay, a collection of 41 minutes, was premiered with 24 dancers. The allure of the evening lay in the "syncopated group dances and balmy romantic duets."[80]

[80] Who Cares? New York City Ballet — www.nycballet.com/discover/ballet-repertory/who-cares

Gershwin

Balanchine had an early opportunity to work with Gershwin on *Goldwyn's Follies*, including a Romeo and Juliet number with a mock duel between ballet-dancing Montagues and tap-dancing Capulets. However, the collaboration did not come for 30 years, so it was only in the '70s that Balanchine choreographed *Who Cares?* to 16 songs composed by Gershwin between 1924 and 1931, all evocative of New York City. Kirstein described the songs and production as a demonstration of "beautiful manners and high style…a body of words and music unblurred by vulgar rhetoric or machine-made sentiment."[81]

In 1972, Balanchine staged his second Stravinsky Festival, choreographing eight new ballets that included the Stravinsky *Violin Concerto*, *Duo Concertantes*, *Symphony in Three Movements*, and *Divertimento* from *La Baiser de la Fée* (Kiss of the Fairy). A one-week intensive celebration of Stravinsky, Balanchine choreographed eight of the 20 world premieres offered, including the *Choral Variations* on Bach's *Vom Himmel Hoch*, *Scherzo a la Russe*, and new versions of *Pulcinella*, co-choreographing with Jerome Robbins.

A 1974 production showed Balanchine at his most experimental, entitled *Variations pour Une Porte et Un Soupir* (Variations on a Door and a Sigh). Balanchine had once described dancers as "poets of gesture."[82] This avant-garde work made much of that observation. A black-caped woman takes the role of a door, a barrier to a male soloist representing a 'sigh.' The work is set to the music of Pierre Henry, which Balanchine heard on a visit to Paris. The work employs the gamut of sounds of human sighing, and the various noises of doors, "creaking, slamming, and swinging on ungreased hinges."[83] The ballet is a pas de deux of 14 variations, in which the dancers' movements are in precise accord with the separate sounds that form the score.

---

[81] Who Cares?

[82] Variations pour une Porte et un Soupir – www.nycballet.com/discover/ballet-repertory/variations-pour-une-porte-et-un-soupir

[83] Variations pour une Porte et un Soupir

As the first ballet of the 1975 season, and the first works of the new Ravel Festival, Balanchine created *Le Tombeau de Couperin* and *Sonatine*. The shorter work, *Sonatine*, was a piano work of Ravel, which Balanchine set for two dancers at 12 minutes of length. The performance marked the 100th anniversary of the composer's birth. Pianist and dancers share the stage.

Sonatine is rarely seen. Perhaps as a nod to the composer's country, Balanchine created the ballet as a pas de deux with onstage violinist for Violette Verdy and Pierre Bonnefoux, two principal dancers born in France. The New York review of *Sonatine* remarked on the changing paradigm of ballet costuming, citing a "different and compelling aura"[84] in which the piece was danced in "a combination of white underwear and World War I vintage tennis clothes."[85]

Le Tombeau de Couperin is a suite of dances in the 18th century French court style for piano, and is distributed between eight couples divided into left and right quadrilles (an 18th century dance form with squadrons at tournaments.) Dancers form geometric patterns – diagonals, diamonds, squares – and dance in unison, mimicking the movements of the opposite quadrille. 'Tombeau' means 'memorial' or 'tomb.' Ravel had

---

[84] New York Times, Balanchine 'Sonatine' Danced in a New Idiom of Costuming –
www.nytimes.com/1978/01/10/archives/balanchine-sonatine-danced-in-mew-idiom-of-costuming.html
[85] New York Times, Sonatine

written a commemorative suite for piano in six movements (prelude, fugue, forlane, minuet, rigaudon and toccata) for six friends who died in World War I. As had the composer, Balanchine incorporated French Baroque style embellishments.

The New York Times review suggested that *Le Tombeau de Couperin* "seems to exist in a dreamy part"[86] of Balanchine's neoclassical world. It is part of the proof that the phrase "stuck in the corps"[87] is not a term often heard at the NYCB. Those who are at the bottom of the company's hierarchy do real dancing, just like their seniors.

On the first program of the festival was *Tzigane*, followed by *Meditation*. The New York Times review suggests that these are not the two works upon which Balanchine should be judged. The first looks like "a Cubist nightclub number of Gypsy motifs, and the second offers an unabashedly sentimental image of a man recalling his lost love."[88] However, in *Tzigane*, the Times declared that "Suzanne Farrell transformed herself into an amazing gypsy – the focus was always on Miss Farrell."[89] It went on to say that the choreography "deliberately recalled the sort of corny gypsy dances that turn up in

[86] Margaret Fuhrer, Contributor, Review: The New York City Ballet's, Beginning with Balanchine, 1/19/2012, Huffpost – www.huffpost.com/entry/review-new-york-city-ballet_b_1214908

[87] Margaret Fuhrer

[88] Jack Anderson, NY Times

[89] Jack Anderson, NY Times

cabarets or operettas. *Tzigane* seemed more than a giddy diversion."[90]

Meditation had been created 12 years earlier for Miss Farrell, an eight-minute pas de deux performed to the music of Tchaikovsky of the same name for violin and piano. The scene is utterly simple. A troubled young man appears and kneels before being approached by a young woman who seeks to console him. They dance together and embrace. She departs, and he is again alone.

The direct opposite type of ballet from *Variations Pour Une Porte et Un Soupir* was created in 1976 with *Coppélia*, branded by many ballet experts as "the happiest ballet in existence."[91] Following the plot of a similar opera, this plot ballet "features a mad inventor and his lifelike mechanical doll, a young man who fancies her…and his resourceful fiancé who saves the day."[92]

Balanchine was presented with the French Légion d'Honneur and was in public standing with both Stravinsky and Picasso. It became clear that he was doing for American dance what the Mariinsky Theater had created for Russia.

The *Chaconne*, set to the music of Christoph Willibald

[90] Jack Anderson, NY Times

[91] Boston Ballet, George Balanchine's Coppélia – www.bostonballet.org/Home/Tickets-Performances/Performances/Coppelia.aspx

[92] Boston Ballet

von Gluck, the early classical opera composer, was created in 1976. Programmed opposite the other-worldly music from *Orfeo* was a jaunty tribute to the British Navy, complete with famous hornpipes and a rousing version of *Rule, Britannia!*

The following year, a four-part *Dance in America Series* for PBS Great Performance was filmed in the city of Nashville. Balanchine traveled with the company for videotaping, and "personally supervised every shot"[93] for the *Vienna Waltzes*. With a strong instinct for the camera, he continually revised steps and angles for compatibility with the medium. In the same year, he choreographed *The Turning Point* pas de deux, among the most powerful cinematic references to classical dance in the art form's history.

Balanchine was nominated for an Emmy Award for participating in the PBS Series *Live from Lincoln Center* in 1978. It was to be his second Emmy nomination, and he won the award on the second try. In the same year, he created *Ballo della Regina* (Dance of the Queen), and *Kammermusik No. 2.*

Ballo della Regina is a neoclassic work set to music cut from Giuseppe Verdi's opera *Don Carlos* in Act III of the original 1877 version. Balanchine, who offered a set of

---

[93] New York City Ballet

variations, was no stranger to opera, having choreographed Bellini's *La Sonnambula* (The Sleepwalker) and *Don Sebastian* of Gaetano Donizetti. He had also choreographed numerous portions of on-stage operatic productions. The variations of *Ballo della Regina* contain a considerable amount of virtuosity and mimic the florid style of the bel canto vocal style.

Kammermusik No. 2 (Chamber music) required "great energy, speed, and precision."[94] With a complicated structure, one dancer likened the work to a computer. It is performed by two couples and an ensemble of eight men. While the ensemble dances to the orchestra, the soloists dance to the intricate passes played by the piano. The score was composed by modern composer Paul Hindemith but references the baroque period. The choreography is marked by "jagged lines and stylized gestures."[95] The New York Times described it as "austere,"[96] adding that the two women dancing side by side "mastered the intricate steps…seem[ingly] as precision-made parts of a perpetual-motion machine."[97]

The creation of composer Robert Schumann's *Davidsbündlertänzer* was premiered in 1980, with a scene from *Waldpurgisnacht* from the opera *Faust* of Charles

[94] Jack Anderson, New York Times, City Ballet: Kammermusik No. 2 – www.nytimes.com/1987/06/09/arts/city-ballet-
kammermusik-no-2.html
[95] Jack Anderson
[96] Jack Anderson
[97] Jack Anderson

Gounod. The Schumann work "takes audiences back to a time of refinement"[98] with dances that imitate the "oft troubled psyche"[99]of Schumann. It stands among his final works and was written to celebrate a reunion with his estranged wife after 16 months. The translation of the title refers to an imaginary society of artists united against the 'philistines' who oppose freedom in the arts.

The *Waldpurgisnacht* was of 17 minutes duration and required 25 dancers. Balanchine had choreographed it for various opera companies, but this was the first entirely danced version. It depicts the devil taking Faust to witness the traditional celebration on the eve of May Day, when souls of the dead freely walk the earth.

The third work created was *Ballade*, set to Gabriel Faure's *Ballade for Piano and Orchestra*, employing 12 dancers at a duration of 13 minutes. A one-movement score for a ballerina and her cavalier, *Ballade* is a series of pas de deux and solos.

The Washington, D.C. premiere of *Ballade* at the Kennedy Center Opera House in 1982 was danced by Merrill Ashley. *The Washington Post* review of the performance suggested that Ashley was among Balanchine's most talented but limited ballerinas. Her

---

[98] New York City Ballet, Robert Schumann's Davidsbündlertänzer – nycballet.com/discover/ballet-repertory/robert-schumann'sdavidsbündlertänzer/

[99] New York City Ballet, Schumann

technique had "lightning speed and rock-solid balances…extraordinary. However, she is the least vulnerable dancer, out of place in romantic roles."[100]

Returning to a work Balanchine choreographed 50 years earlier for Les Ballets, the 1981 Tchaikovsky Festival of New York City Ballet presented a new version of *Mozartiana,* Mozart works to Tchaikovsky arrangements. The opening section is a 'preghiera' (prayer) followed by a Gigue, Minuet, Theme and Variations and a 'Finale.' The preghiera calls for the prima ballerina accompanied by four young girls, set to the exquisite *Ave Verum Corpus* of Mozart. The male soloist dances the Gigue, and four women from the corps take the Minuet. The male and female soloists join for a classical pas de deux in a set of variations, and the entire cast reunites for the finale. The piece is 28 minutes of duration and calls for 7 dancers in all.

In 1981, Balanchine resurrected a ballet he had first created at the age of 21, redesigning his *L'enfant et les Sortileges*, with music by Maurice Ravel. With an increasingly modern technology, he was able to use special effects, including animation on the set of the story. It was premiered in a famous telecast on May 25, 1981. In an odd choice for a story for dance, a boy becomes

---

[100] Alexandra Tomalonis, Washington Post, Balanchine's Ballade, Oct. 8, 1982 –
    weww.washingtonpost.com/archive/lifestyle/1982/1-/05/balanchine's-ballade

spellbound as his possessions come to life. The "defiant little boy is hurled into an anthropomorphic world of threatening objects and creatures."[101] *L'enfant et les Sortileges* is a ballet only in the formal sense. There are few set dance sequences, and the singers are as prominent at furthering the plot as are the dancers. As a television classic, the Ravel/Balanchine effort rivals Gian Carlo Menotti's *Amahl and the Night Visitors.*

In 1982, Balanchine directed another series of Stravinsky's works with the NYCB. In a 9-day festival of Stravinsky's music for his Centennial Celebration, the strongest was saved for the final concert. Balanchine and Stravinsky continued to act as fellow risk-takers. Both were born in Russia, were both naturally innovative and "widely considered masters of their art forms who have endured the test of time."[102] Charles M. Joseph wrote, "Balanchine employed his choreography as a conduit through which the message of Stravinsky's music could be clarified and strengthened."[103]

The staging was "unsettling"[104] for those who came to see only dance. None existed in the first piece at all, rather it was a vocal cantata entitled *Zvezdoliki* sung by 20 male

[101] John J. O'Connor, TV: Balanchine's 'Spellbound Child', May 25, 1981, New York Times – www.nytimes.com/1981/05/25/arts/tv-balanchine-s-spellbound-child.html

[102] Anna Kisselgoff, Dance: 'Persephone' Staged by Balanchine, June 20, 1982 – www.nytimes.com/1982//06/20arts/dance-persephone-staged-by-balanchine.html

[103] Anna Kisselgoff, Persephone

[104] Anna Kisselgoff, Persephone

members of the New York City Opera Chorus. Then came *Persephone*. The score was composed for Ida Rubinstein's ballet company in 1933. Nature is the theme of the melodrama, and the signature quality of its leading lady. As "a symbol for Spring,"[105] Persephone is abducted to Hades, but allowed to replenish the Earth on a semi-annual basis. Dance portions came mainly in groups of three pas de deux for Mel Tomlinson's Pluto and Miss Arnoldinger's Persephone. Gen Horiuchi, later director of the St. Louis ballet, "flashes through brilliantly in a solo for Mercury."[106]

George Balanchine died in New York City on April 30, 1983 at the age of 79. He had been taken to Roosevelt Hospital due to pneumonia that arose from a progressive neurological disorder, but despite his age, Balanchine's dancers reacted with shock to his death, as he still seemed strong to them. Many dancers at the company noted that during coaching, Balanchine often "did the steps more beautifully than they did.[107] Regardless of the fact that he was old or dressed in Western style, "he always outclassed them."[108]

At the time of his death, Balanchine was widely regarded as the man who "elevated ballet to an independent art."[109]

---

[105] Anna Kisselgoff, Persephone

[106] Anna Kisselgoff, Persephone

[107] Joan Acocella, Balanchine Teaching, Jan. 11, 2019, New Yorker – www.newyorker.com/culture/culture-desk/balanchine-teaching

[108] Joan Acocella

He once said that music was so closely related to dance that his work became "an invitation to see the music and hear the dancing."[110] When compared to Petipa, well-meaning or not, he was flattered for being included in such a lineage, calling Petipa his "spiritual father."[111] Fellow choreographers and dancers made note that he danced the same steps as Petipa, but at "perilous angles…and at a speed that could exist only in the 20th century."[112]

The old Russian and European 'museum concept' was entirely ruled out for the new American company. Its uniqueness was to be built on the fact that the company performed its own works, not an endless thread of 19th century classics and revivals. Balanchine ran his company with a much-celebrated "no-star policy,"[113] which included himself. He observed that "as soon as you start selling a person, that's commercial."[114]

An anti-romantic, Balanchine mystified the ballet world by treating romantic themes with great tenderness. In an instant, he would take the marches of John Philip Sousa, a jazz or cowboy tune. Being a pure American in his later years, he kept his fondness for Russian Easter cake, which

---

[109] Anna kisselgoff, New York Time, George Balanchine, 79, Dies in New York, 1983 – www.nytimes.com
[110] Anna Kisselgoff, New York Times
[111] Anna Kisselgoff
[112] Anna Kisselgoff
[113] Anna Kisselgoff
[114] Anna Kisselgoff

he loved to make himself. He learned American slang with a passion, but never lost his distinct Russian accent. He could mimic from memory any television commercial, and American popular culture was thoroughly familiar to him. All told, the authoritative catalogue of his works lists 465 created by Balanchine in his career. In a great display of eclecticism, he crossed literally every genre imaginable, including musical theater and operetta. Film credits included *Star-Spangled Banner, I Was an Adventuress*, and *Goldwyn Follies*. Along with these were numerous ballets for opera productions and television, a new medium at the time for which he created several specific works. In his most creative works, he generally de-emphasized the plot, preferring to let "dance be the star of the show."[115] Within moments of productions, however, he could alternate between being "the hopeless romantic, classicist, intellectual modernist."[116]

Respect for Balanchine was absolute within the company. "We are under the dictatorship of one man, whom we adore and respect, and his every whim is our law, no questions asked,"[117] said Susan Bordo, author of *Reading the Ballerina's Body*.

Balanchine's "presence was so dominant at NYCB that

[115] New York City Ballet

[116] New York City Ballet

[117] Susan Bordo, Reading the Ballerina's Body: Susan Bordo Shed Light on Anastasia Volochkova and HeidiGunthere, *Dance Research Journal*, Vol. 37 No. 2 (Winter, 2005)

dancers, scenic preparation, the music investiture all seem to operate within the same system," [118] even in ballets not choreographed by him. The New York City Ballet's mission was to "annihilate history…to canonize the new."[119] The company strove to avoid the pitfall of repeating performances multiple times, avoiding "staleness and mechanical delivery…by keeping old works as if they were new."[120] Balanchine's company credo was to invent ways in which the dancers could surpass themselves. What only Edward Villella could do years before, "boys in the corps can to today."[121]

Balanchine's dancers have an individual look and way of dancing. Everyone on the stage dances like a soloist, a habit which often evokes criticism of the company. Houston and Basel have neater lines, but New York excites in an uncommon way. The corps is not employed as a single immense body, but couple by couple, small group by small group. In New York, the audience comes to learn the names of the corps members. There is an interaction between soloists, ensemble and music, rather than a star out front with a large accompanying body.

The de-emphasizing of "stars" was part of Balanchine's belief that 19th century ballet had lost much of its prestige,

---

[118] Marcia B. Siegel, George Balanchine, 1904-1983, *The Hudson Review* Vol. 36 No. 3 (Autumn, 1983)

[119] Marcia B. Siegel

[120] Marcia B. Siegel

[121] Marcia B. Siegel

a "prestige that resided with the reputation of the famous dancers."[122] The individual personality of dancers and some directors was ever present, but to the outer world, glory was given to few choreographers. Even in the early 20th century, the renown in dance was attached to the dancers rather than to the dance. The reputations of Pavlova, Nijinsky, Karsavina, and Bakst, Stravinsky, and Picasso "overwhelmed the pattern of the dancers."[123]

In the mid-20th century, Balanchine did something entirely without precedent. He "founded a school, a style, a company, and a repertory"[124] that was not only local, but national and international, all from scratch. He depended little on poets, libretti, or practical pretexts, and yet filled the choreography with much poetry. He preferred to light a dancer rather than to clothe her in "sumptuous applied decorations."[125] "Physical action, neither color nor pantomime determines the poetry inherent in any given Balanchine work – he loves aristocratic leanness."[126] In the short span of 20 years, Balanchine took American-born dancers and "molded them into his ideally plastic material…their inbred predilection for sport, their aptitude for running, jumping and diving."[127]

---

[122] Lincoln Kirstein, The Position of Balanchine, *Salmagundi* No. 33/34 Dance (Spring-Summer 1976), Skidmore College

[123] Lincoln Kirstein

[124] Lincoln Kirstein

[125] Lincoln Kirstein

[126] Lincoln Kerstein

[127] Lincoln Kirstein

Even in Broadway theaters and film, Balanchine decried what he called "calculated vulgarity"[128] and likens a ballet program "to the menu of a great restaurant."[129] His artistic procedure has given a new importance to dance composition, and "he has extended the boundaries of useful styles…made the craft and career of choreographers easier for young dancers and choreographers who are following him."[130]

"Through-line" dancing marks Balanchine's style, a continuous motion along with the music, as with the melody. Baryshnikov had a significant amount of trouble with this after joining the New York City Ballet, after having been a Bolshoi-style "stop and go"[131] dancer.

Despite his great respect for women as dancers, he had little for them in the way of administrators. He gave his company over to Peter Martin when he had a line of top professional women who, according to one former dancer, could have done it far better. Martins inaugurated his run at NYCB by inexplicably firing the great Suzanne Farrell, a super-talent, according to dancer Judith Johnson.

Today, the New York City Ballet typically performs for 23 weeks out of the year and is still housed in the $30 million dollar David H. Hoch Theater, funded by the city

---

[128] Lincoln Kirstein

[129] Lincoln Kirstein

[130] Lincoln Kirstein

[131] Lincoln Kirstein

and state. The theater has now been opened for 60 years, with the Saratoga Performing Arts Center serving as the company's permanent summer home for nearly as long. The New York City Ballet has offered numerous appearances in European capitals. World performances have taken the company to Australia, China, Brazil, South Korea, and Taiwan. It has made three historic trips to Russia and to the major cities of the U.S. and Canada.

Today, Balanchine's brainchild sports a roster of 90 dancers, making it the largest dance organization in the United States. Of the standard repertory of over 150 works, the majority were originally choreographed by Balanchine and Robbins. Following Balanchine's death in 1983, Robbins and Martin shared the title of Ballet Master in Chief. In 2009, Katherine Brown was named the first Executive Director of the company. In February of 2019, Jonathan Stafford was named the new Artistic Director of both the ballet company and the school. Wendy Whelan was named Associate Artistic Director of the company at the same time.

Despite his classical Russian background, Balanchine remained forward-thinking and innovative, continuing to absorb diverse cultural phenomena into his company and its choreography. As he observed on multiple occasions, "I don't have a past. I have a continuous present. The past is part of the present, just as the future is – we exist in time"[132] His bent toward innovative collaborations was affirmed by his belief that dance "is a continuation. You cannot predict the signs of its evolution."[133]

Online Resources

Other books about 20th century history by Charles River Editors

Further Reading

Acocella, Joan, Balanchine Teaching, Jan. 11, 2017, New Yorker – www.newyorker.com/culture/culture-desk/balanchine-teaching

Adler Reba, Two Versions of Barabau, *Dance Chronicle*, Vol. 4 No. 4 (1981)

Agon, The George Balanchine Trust – www.balanchine.com/Ballet/Agon

Allegro Brillante, The George Balanchine Trust – www.balanchine.com/Ballet/Allegro-Brillante

Anderson Jack, New York Times, City Ballet: Kammermusik No. 2 – www.nytimes.com/1987/06/09/arts/city-ballet-kammermusik-no-2.html

Boston Ballet, George Balanchine's Coppélia –

---

[132] The George Balanchine Trust

[133] The George Balanchine Trust

www.bostonballet.org/Home/Tickets-Performances/Performances/Coppelia.aspx

Bourée Fantastique, NYBC – www.nycballet.co/discover/ballet-repertory/bouree-fantastique

Brahms-Schoenberg Quartet – www.balanchine.com/Ballet/Brahms-Schoenberg-Quartet

Bugaku. The George Balanchine Trust – www.balanchine.com/Ballet/Bugaku

Craft, Robert, Stravinsky and Balanchine, New York Review Oct. 8, 1998 – www.nybooks.com/articles/1998/stravinsky-balanchine/

Episodes, The George Balanchine Trust – www.balanchine.com/Ballet/Episodes

Fuhrer, Margaret, Contributor, Review: New York City Ballet, Beginning with Balanchine, 1/19/2012, Huffpost – www.huffpost.com./entry/review-new-york-city-ballet_b_1214908

George Balanchine.s The Nutcracker, George Balanchine Trust – www.balanchine.com/George-Balanchine's-The-Nutcracker

Homans, Jennifer, Balanchine: Making and Being Don Quixote, The New York Review, June 4, 2015 –

www.nybooks.com/articles/2015/06/04/balanchine-making-being-don-quixote

IMDB, Sergei Diaghilev – www.imdb.com/nm/1959850

IMDB, Tamara Tamounova (1919-1996) – www.imdb.com/name/nm0869565/

Kisselgoff, Anna, New York Times, George Balanchine, 79, Dies in New York, May 1, 1983 – www.nytimes.com/1983/05/01/obituaries/george-balanchine-79-dies-in-new-york.html

Kisselgoff, AnnaNew York Times, The Dance: 'Episodes,' June 1, 1986 – www.nytimes.com/1986/06.01/arts/the-dance-episodes.html

Kisselgoff, Anna Dance: 'Persephone' Staged by Balanchine, June 20, 1982 – www.nytimes.com/1982//06/20arts/dance-persephone-staged-by-balanchine.html

Jewels, The George Balanchine Trust – www.balanchine.com/Ballet/Jewels

Kirstein, Lincoln: The Position of Balanchine, *Salmagundi*, No. 33/34 (Spring-Summer 1976) Skidmore College

Liebeslieder Walzer, The George Balanchine Trust –

www.balanchine.com/Ballet/Liebeslieder-Walzer

Lyopukhov, Fyodor, Soviet Choreographer, Britannica – Britannica.com/biography/Fyodor-Lopukhov

Midsummer Night's Dream, The George Balanchine Trust – www.balanchine.com/Ballet/A-Midsummer-Night's-Dream

Movements for Piano and Orchestra, NY City Ballet – www.nycballet.com/discover-ballet-repertory/movements-for-piano-and-orchestra

National Endowment for the Humanities, George Balanchine and the United States, (Jan/Feb 2016 Vol. 37 No 1) HUMANITIES

New York City Ballet, Robert Schumann's Davidsbündlertänzer – nycballet.com/discover/ballet-repertory/robert-schumann'sdavidsbündlertänzer/

New York City Ballet, George Balanchine – www.nycballet.com/discover/out-history/george-balanchine

New York City Ballet, Tchaikovsky Pas de Deux, - www.nycballet.com/discover/ballet-repertory/tschaikovsky-pas-de-deux

New York Times, Balanchine 'Sonatine' Danced in a New Idiom of Costuming –

www.nytimes.com/1978/01/10/archives/balanchine-sonatine-danced-in-mew-idiom-of-costuming.html

The New Yorker, Balanchine Teaching – www.newyorker.com/culture/culture-desk/balanchine-teaching

NYCB, Our History – www.nycballet.com/discover/our-history/

O'Connor, John J. TV: Balanchine's 'Spellbound Child', May 25, 1981, New York Times – www.nytimes.com/1981/05/25/arts/tv-balanchine-s-spellbound-child.html

Prodigal Son, George Balanchine Trust – www.balanchine.com/Ballet/Prodigal-Son/

SAB, School of American Ballet – www.sab.org/tyhe-school-and-nycb/

San Francisco Ballet, Balanchine and Stravinsky: An Innovative Partnership – www.sfballet.org/balanchine-and-stravinsky-an-innovative-partnership/

Scotch Symphony, NYCB – www.nycballet.com/discover/ballet-repertory/scoth-symphony

Siegel, Marcia B., George Balanchine, 1904-1983, *The Hudson Review* Vol. 36 No. 3 (Autumn 1983)

Square Dance, The George Balanchine Trust – www.balanchine.com/Ballet/Square-Dance

Stars and Stripes, The George Balanchine Trust – www.balanchine.com/Stars-and-Stripes

Symphony in C, The George Balanchine Trust – www.balanchine.com/Ballet/Symphony-in-C

The Blog @ The Barre, Stars and Stripes, 7/18/2021 – www.theballetspot.com/the-blog-the-barre/george-balanchine-stars-and-stripes-a-brief-history-of-the-ballet

The George Balanchine Trust, George Balanchine – www.balanchine.com/george-balanchine

The George Balanchine Trust, Apollo – www.balanchine.com/Ballet/Apollo

The Marius Petipa Society – www.petipasociety.com/about/

The New Yorker, Balanchine Said – www.newyorker.com/magazine/2009/01.06/balanchine-said

Tomalonis Alexandra, Washington Post, Balanchine's Ballade, Oct. 8, 1982 – weww.washingtonpost.com/archive/lifestyle/1982/1-/05/balanchine's-ballade

Variations pour une Porte et un Soupir – www. –
www.nycballet.com/discover/ballet-repertory/variations-
pour-une-porte-et-un-soupir

Walker, Katherine Sorley, George Balanchine, Russian-
American Choreographer, Britannica –
www.britannice.com/biography/George-Balanchine

Who Cares? New York City Ballet –
www.nycballet.com/discover/ballet-repertory/who-cares